Never Again

Ketakee

NEVER AGAIN
Ketakee

© Ketakee

Published in 2024

© Published by

Qurate Books Pvt. Ltd.
Goa 403523, India
www.quratebooks.com
Tel: 1800-210-6527, Email: info@quratebooks.com

ISBN: 978-93-58983-41-8

Introduction

Love is a vast and complex collage, woven with threads of emotion that goes beyond the boundaries of words. It cannot be confined to a single definition, nor fully captured in any one language. Like the myriad tongues spoken across the globe, love, too, has its own dialects—each offering a unique expression of the heart's deepest desires and affections.

In this collection, titled *Never Again*, love is explored in its many forms, unfolding through the beauty of language.

As you journey through these pages, you will encounter the tender whispers of romance, the passionate cries of longing, and the quiet, enduring presence of love that defies time. Each poem serves as a reminder that love, in all its forms, is a universal experience, yet one that is deeply personal and profoundly shaped by the words we choose to express it.

Never Again invites you to explore the rich and varied landscape of love, offering a glimpse into the ways this powerful emotion is experienced and articulated. Through the interplay of language and feeling, this collection seeks to reveal that, while love may be universal, its expression is as diverse and boundless as the human heart itself.

About the Author

Ketakee, a pragmatic individual, is remarkably clear about her thoughts, goals, and life objectives. Her professional journey began with a glamorous role in the aviation industry. Over time, she comfortably expanded her experience across diverse fields such as hospitality, corporate management, and education. This multifaceted career, coupled with her love for exploring the world and meeting new people, has shaped her into a unique and versatile personality. A fun-loving individual with vibrant layers to her character, Ketakee embodies love across the many roles she plays: mother, wife, daughter, friend, and lover.

The sudden departure of loved ones from her life led her through a near-traumatic experience. In her process of healing, she found inspiration within herself, unveiling a new sense of "ME." Through introspection, she began expressing herself in poetry, blending emotions of love, inspiration, elation, sorrow, abandonment, and resentment. These sentiments resonate in her previous works, *A Thread Between You and Me and Whispered Verses: Echoes of the Soul.*

Never Again is her endeavor to explore the hidden desires within a woman—aspirations that remained unfulfilled due to personal and societal constraints. In defiance of life's insolent setbacks and to be a beacon of hope for those wishing to live authentically, she penned *Never Again.* Each poem unveils a part of the journey toward self-discovery, inviting readers to connect with their inner selves and hidden dreams. This work has the potential to transform readers into sensitive yet practical individuals, strengthening their understanding of interpersonal dynamics within relationships.

The poems reflect the author's thoughts, but each reader is encouraged to form their own interpretations and judgments. Ketakee welcomes feedback from readers, as their insights inspire her to continue creating meaningful poetry.

You can write on: panditurvil7@gmail.com

Beginning

The game of pretension
Is finally concluded.
I distinguished between—
The Truth and The Concocted!

Beneath those joyful, serene eyes,
Deep-hidden sadness lay,
Uncovered by a tender touch,
True feelings found their way.

A smile took away the misery
From those who seemed the happiest;
Their facades of joy shattered,
Revealing hearts in distress.

This new beginning, surreal yet true,
Leads in a positive way;
A life of authenticity blooms,
Unaffected, here to stay.

Choice

The rumbling of my belly
Indicated something scary.

Relentless thoughts
of all sorts
Clogged my brain
with a tremendous strain.

Stuck between two worlds,
Happy or sad, which to unfurl?
I cannot choose,
or choose to refuse,
The pain in the stress,
creating a mess.

Reason

This day,
A new dawn for a boy,
Oblivious of the reason
To be here,
In this sphere.

Days passed by,
Months went by,
Years passed as well,
Without knowing
The rationale of his life.

He ushered in his journey
For me.
I, unaware of our story,
Followed my heart;
A call was enough
To get him close.
The way he appeared
Was astonishing,
For sure.

He was born
To share those moments
That are cherished forever.

He was born
To live those moments
Which he owned for a reason.

He was born
To be with me forever
And not for a season.

He is born
To be loved,
To be pampered,
To be cherished,
And to be mine for eternity.

Hope

I need to be lost,
forever in his embrace.

I wish to seize his heart,
like no one ever has before.

I need to be adored by him,
as no one has ever adored anybody else.

I basically trust to remain by his side
until my final breath;
one pledge to stand.

Confession

The confession of his love
Breathed into me a quiet strength,
A courage to face the world,
To stand firm and grow stronger.

In the sanctuary of his love,
I discovered a profound solace,
An invincible core,
Unfathomable to others.

We engaged in endless discussions
Of a future together, forever intertwined.
He held his convictions,
And I clung to mine.
Yet in conjunction,
We decided to shine.

The Eyes

The tranquil eyes
Gazed at me,
With a smile
That melted me!

It was a pleasure
To behold this sight
When he clasped my arm
And held it tight.

He showered his love upon me
And embraced all my worries.
He exactly knew
What I am going through.

Desire

Tears spurts from his eyes
As he listens to my despair,
Yet he claims indifference to the world.

He whines in anguish,
Witnessing my pain,
Yet he affirms ignorance of love.

He longs to whisk me away
From the sorrows of life,
Yet he speaks of parting paths.

So I desire to ask:
Will you truly take me away?
For in the shelter of your love,
I seek my endless stay,
Where shadows of devotion
Gently cradle me each day.

Bond

My eyes wait desperately for a glimpse of him,
And the comforting smile he always sends my
way.

My heart eagerly anticipates the unspoken
connection
That binds us deeply beyond mere words.

My body aches for his tender touch,
Melting me away in his warm embrace.

I wish for this bond to last forever,
For I cannot envisage my life
Even for a moment without him.

The Chase

They tried to pull me down,
But I bounced back,
Forgetting the frown.

Today, I realized
Nothing in the world
Can block my chase,
For I am chasing myself
In this race!

A Nameless Bond

Who are we?
What are we?
We cannot say.
Together, yet undefined,
We have no name for this bond we share!

Not bound by nuptial ties,
Yet close as consorts;
No walls of silence or sighs,
Yet we are nameless!

Not lovers lost in the fever of youth,
Yet we savor the sweetness of every touch,
Indulging in love's many shades
Without a label to frame our closeness!

No vows taken to last a lifetime,
Yet a discrete thread binds us—
An unwritten fact we are,
As we wander without a name!

So we stay—something more than friends,
Something less profound than a verdict of
fate,
An unconditional bond in the land of titles,
Happily contented to just be in our lovable
space!

Silent Fear

A silent fear grips me with unease,
Anxiety creeping, its origin unknown,
But hold sudden and firm.

Fear of the known,
Fear of my own,
Suddenly a stranger
Who's turned cold.

Trying to mend things,
He discovers ideas,
While I remain untouched
And an indifferent being.

How do I express?
How do I change?
Love around me now
Has a new name—
A name that nurtures,
A name that pampers,
A name that's mine,
A name that's forever divine!

Vows

I now comprehend the reason
For the boundless love I hold for you.

Those eyes, shimmering with light,
Yet urging for the embrace of affection.

That smile, radiating pure bliss,
Yet craving for a touch of true joy.

The "You" who appears complete,
Yet harbors an emptiness deep within.

I vow to love you endlessly,
Even if that love is never returned.

Assurance

In a world full of chaos,
I promise to bring you peace.
You can give me all your worries,
And let your troubles cease.

In a place where trust is rare,
I'll be someone you can rely on.
I won't break any promises;
As long as I'm here, they'll stay strong.

When things feel dark and hopeless,
I'll bring a bright smile to your day,
Like a butterfly full of color,
Chasing dreams along the way.

Let me be the light in your darkness,
The hope when things seem blue.
Let me bring that joy to your face,
The kind that shines through.

Because your smile lights up my day,
And it brightens the world in its own way.

A Moment

A gloomy commencement,
Tears sprinting; blazing cheeks—
Shattered weeping!

Heart with placid emotions,
Unknown of the direction,
Awaiting the moment,
Someone to embrace at once.

He enlightened my conscience
To treasure my valuation,
Estimated by self
And not by others' calculation!

Together

Life is a journey, bound by thresholds,
Set by others, for others.
But I chose to break them all.
You held me close, saved me from the fall.
Cradling the child within me,
You lifted me and set me free.

Together we walk, hand in hand,
Building our world, where love expands.
With every step, in joy or sorrow,
We find strength in each other for tomorrow.

All I seek now
Is the smile on your face,
That makes me go, "Wow."
Your smallest gestures
Illuminate my entire day,
In every little way.

Embrace

Whenever I hug you,
my entire universe settles between your arms.

In that embrace,
I feel a shield of protection,
where no harm can reach me.

My heart races alongside yours,
finding peace at its very core.
Every beat of our hearts aligns perfectly,
creating a rhythm words can't capture.

My mind becomes still,
no longer reacting to the world outside.
There is a quiet relief as every ounce of burden
dissolves,
and my heart leaps from my chest to yours.

In those moments, when I hold you close,
the world becomes ours.
My soul journeys from the stars to the earth,
lost, yet utterly found, in your embrace.

Solace

Struggling to survive,
I find myself enmeshed
In the toil of daily life.

Eyes watch my every move,
Scrutinizing, anticipating
What my next step will be.

Freedom is granted,
Yet I remain confined
Within invisible boundaries.

I desire to break free,
To defy the norms,
Live life to the fullest
With a cool, obstinate smile.

For solace, I find,
Is in your embrace—
A haven amidst the storm.

Stolen Moment

A stolen moment,
Worth more than anything in this world.

It brings a happiness
Known only to those who've felt it.

It offers a solace
That can only be truly lived.

It grants a peace
That can only be experienced.

This feeling, understood only by you and me,
While the rest of the world
Remains oblivious to its divinity.

Drawn Away

The queen of the waves
Forgot how to stay afloat.

The doyenne of the land
Mislaid her sense of worth.

The once-proud princess
Forsook the courage for her battles.

The joy within her soul
Has come to its close,
As she is drawn away,
Untethered from her mate.

Messed Up

A glimpse of unease
Made him unsettled—
Who will mend the wounds
That he inflicted?

The sorrow on my face
Erased his fleeting smile—
How can I find my own,
When he's stolen it away?

The turmoil in my mind
Shattered his joyful thoughts—
How can I piece myself together
When he's left me messed up?

Misunderstood

I showed I cared; I tried my best,
But my concern became a test.
What I gave with an open heart
Felt like nagging from the start.

Each time I spoke,
It pushed him further, far away.
My love, I thought, soft like gentle rain,
Was something seen as pain.

How can caring go so wrong
When all I wanted was to belong?
Now I stand with feelings bruised,
Unsure, confused, and so accused.

I believed my love would make them see,
But it feels like a weight, not free.
What was warmth was considered strain;

Turmoil

There's such a turmoil inside me,
A discussion with my conscience.
Why do I love him so deeply
When he's not even destined to be mine?

Why is he so adamant,
Refusing to give us a chance?
Why has he set so many barriers?
Can't he just love me with a sigh?

Should we make a vow,
Or let things be as they are?
Will we stay together,
Or will these conditions tear us apart?

Tempest

Drowned in profound thoughts,
My soul yearns for answers
To questions that linger—
Unspoken, yet meant to remain unanswered.

This tempest within, this inner turmoil,
Erodes me slowly,
Breeding self-doubt,
Chipping away at my sense of worth, bit by
bit.

Is it the fear of an unknown stranger,
Or the dread of losing you?
My heart, caught in the crossfire,
Pushes one away while drawing you closer still.

I will be undone
If we are to part like night and day.
Let the bond between us endure,
For it is you I strive for, the one I hold dear.

Distance

I can feel the distance;
I can sense the strain—
An intolerable weight,
Pulling me down again and again.

I can hear the silence,
Where words once filled the air.
The load of your absence dawdles,
A void I cannot bear.

The light in your eyes fades,
Like dusk overtakes the sky.
Without you here beside me,
I'm left to wonder why.

Trace

A Glance
That reshaped my world.

A Smile
That infused peace into my life.

A Hand
That held me like never before.

A Touch
That kindled a grin on my face.

He awakened my soul
With just a simple embrace;
He brightened my world
And left an indelible trace.

Unanswered

The cold weather on the outside,
But a warm storm inside.

"How did you land up here?"
Asked my heart, in fear.

Is it because of someone,
Or for someone?
Yet to be answered!

My heart longed for answers,
Yet all in vain;
Waiting for the moment
When clarity would dawn upon my soul
To finally serve my life well!

Absence

His absence created an emptiness,
A silence that echoed louder than words.
I missed the sound of his laughter,
The warmth of his voice,
Filling the empty spaces around me,
Reminding me of how lonely I was today.

I truly wanted his mischief,
The kind that left me breathless,
The playful chaos I pretended to resist.

The memory of his kisses and tender embraces
Clung to my skin,
Sending a shrill shiver
That lasted forever!

His touch lingered in every part of me,
A haunting presence that stirred my mind.
And in the quiet of this day,
I craved him more than ever,
Hoping to find him again,
Even in the echoes of my heart!

Pain

This strange ache of loving someone,
Yet being unable to share,
Is slowly tearing me apart.

So much I wish to say,
But a nameless fear
Keeps me silent.

I don't want to overwhelm him
With my thoughts,
But I long to speak so much.

Is there a way to find the words?
Will the one I need to speak with
Truly understand?

He

His Gaze
Sets my blood dancing in my veins,
Unveiling my deepest desires for romance.

His Grin
Dispels the pessimism in my mind,
Reassuring me that we are intertwined.

His Fragrance
Is the only pheromone I desire;
In his embrace is everything I acquire.

His Touch
Is the only divine feeling,
For it has helped me in complete healing.

I yearn for him to be mine forever,
Driven by my selfish desire to be together.

Broken

The moment I feared
Arrived without warning,
Leaving me broken,
And my world in mourning.

This wasn't the path
I had envisioned to take,
But who can bend destiny
Or alter what fate will make?

I couldn't keep him close;
He slipped away once more.
Now I'm left alone,
With guilt I cannot ignore.

Fear

The dark night,
The silent streets,
Enjoying the buzz
That's off-beat.

The shady sky,
The hidden moon,
Cherishing the time,
For it won't be here soon.

A loud shout, I could hear
Within me, saying,
"Do not fear!"

Realization

A heart of gold,
A smile that unfolds,
The griefs suffered,
Yet never muttered.

A strong hope,
Dangling like a rope,
For everyone to hold
And narrate the untold.

An ever-giving hand,
Like a magic wand,
That would always share
Without the world's care.

Found

The sun converged
In the endless horizon,
Leaving me submerged
In contemplation.

A tempest of notions
Probing my acumen,
Until a glorious response
I finally obtain.

No Matter What

This feeling tickles me,
A gift so tender, given by thee.

A moment of delight,
Cherished to the greatest height.

Yet a little worry haunts me,
Soon, thou wilt be afar, beyond seven seas.

Seal a promise, to be together;
No matter the distance,
We'll be the best companions—forever.

Amour

It is not love
That holds us together,
But respect and understanding
That do!

It is not pity
That strengthens our bond,
But care
That does!

Loving you is a joy;
Being loved by you, a satisfaction.
Caring for you is a pleasure;
Being cared for by you, a benediction.

Untold Poetry

Loving you is beyond words!

It's like
The rhythm of the waves, the endless sky,
A serene sunrise,
With birds on the horizon that fly.

In your embosom, I feel complete.
Your voice is home to me.

Us: an unpublished poetry, untold and
intimate,
Only deciphered by you and me.

Deserve

I loved,
Hoping to be loved in return.

I cared,
Wishing to be cared for.

I smiled,
Longing to be smiled at.

I cried,
Yearning to be cried for.

Yet, all my efforts seemed in vain,
When the love I sought,
And the pain I endured,
Brought no reward.

But then, a sudden ray of hope,
A chance to cope,
As I realized—
He loves me,
Just as I once loved.

Now, I wonder,
Am I giving him back
The love he truly deserves?

Freedom

A girl, confined for years,
Yet unaware of her cage,
For she knew not the world beyond,
Nor the freedom outside her walls.

Then came a man, strong and kind,
Who saw her as more than she'd ever known.
He led her gently to a new path,
To live, to laugh, to survive.

But in her fear, she built new walls around
him,
Demanding his presence always.
He gave, and she received.
Trapped now, not by her walls,
But by her unyielding needs.

Realizing her folly, she spoke with a tear,
"I'll no longer bind you, my love, I swear.
Fly free as you once did; no chains will remain,
For in your freedom, I'll find peace again."

The End

Lying in bed,
Engrossed in a thousand thoughts,
My mind tossed in darkness
On the notions of every sought.

Twisting and turning,
Overhauling the beliefs
Which once were
A sort of relief.

At once,
The murk vanished
When the curtains unmasked,
Letting the sunshine land on me.
Giving a drift,
Laying a trail,
And illustrating—
Every dark cloud has a silver lining,
Without fail.

Lost Love

His lost love has returned,
Claiming the past should be revived.
He assured me of his feelings,
But now, what does his heart truly decide?

I don't wish to stand in the way,
Knowing there's no future in us.
Why be the cause of his dismay,
Or an obstacle to his happiness?

Yet, it stings as I find myself here,
Offering advice for him to reunite,
Urging him to grant her a second chance,
To embrace a fresh start and reconcile.

But in the quiet corners of my mind,
The ache remains, an unspoken plea.
For though I let him go with grace,
The loss weighs heavy, still haunting me.

Peace of Mind

In this hectic world,
Embracing the sunshine
Rejuvenated me!

In the bustling street,
Holding your hands
Solaced me!

In the grey world,
Full of pessimism,
The twinkle in your eye
Propelled me!

Tired and occupied,
I am always snowed with things,
Desperately in search of peace,
Which is impossible, it seems.

My peace of mind...
I finally found.
It was in YOU!
Now I realize.

Silence

A weird sensation
Holds me tight,
Whipping my core
And twisting my gut.

This unavoidable silence,
This frightening distance,
An inconsolable pain
That wears me down.

My heart cries
To see you.
Unbearably,
I keep missing you!

Craving

I crave for him
Like a child for his toy,
And he longs for me,
Like the eyes for slumber's joy.

I hanker for him
Like a mother for her child,
And he waits for me,
Like the moon for night, soft and mild.

I ache for him
Like a bird for the open sky,
And he seeks my touch,
Like the sun seeks the horizon high.

I pine for him
Like a flower for the morning dew,
And he finds solace in me,
Like the stars in the midnight blue.

Forever

A seed teaches us to grow in silence,
Buried deep, yet close to love,
Changing form, but never apart.

A flower blooms and fades;
Its fragrance lingers like your touch,
Bringing joy that only I know.

A tree stands through every storm,
Offering shelter despite its pain,
Just as your love holds me, strong and true.

And in your arms, I find my peace—
A love so deep, so pure, so kind,
Forever cherished, forever mine.

Web

My heart sinks, my mind is fraught,
With whispers of another's thought.
The fear that someone else may claim
The love I hold and call his name.

I stand so helpless, torn apart,
Unable to voice what's in my heart.
To ask if she has won his grace,
Or if I still hold that very place.

It pains me deep, a silent cry,
To find another's warmth and care,
While I am left with shadows there.

I feel lost in this cruel game,
Wondering if he'll still utter my name.
If not my future, is she his fate?
Should I wait and not let these thoughts set?

Caught in this web, I cannot bear;
I crave for "us," a "so-called forever."
But if forever slips away,
Will I have the strength to walk away?

Prop

A beautiful heart
That got wind of the fact:
Nothing in this world
Is enduring and intact.

It tried doping out
In every possible way,
Yet couldn't decipher
How to freely slay.

To convulse forever
Has to stop,
If one has to be in mirth
And not somebody's prop!

Together

Life is a journey, bound by thresholds,
Set by others, for others.
But I chose to break them all.
You held me close, saved me from the fall,
Cradling the child within me.
You lifted me and set me free.

Together we walk, hand in hand,
Building our world, where love expands.
With every step, in joy or sorrow,
We find strength in each other for tomorrow.

All I seek now
Is the smile on your face that makes me go,
"Wow!"
Your smallest gestures
Illuminate my entire day,
In every little way.

Love

With sealed lips, I gesture emotions,
Overwhelming every thought.

With closed eyes, I envision a future,
Almost beyond reach.

With bound hands, I stretch out to you,
Yearning for an embrace once more.

With reluctant feet,
I tread against the current, still caught in the
opposite tide.

With a wounded heart, I continue to love you,
No matter the circumstance.

Unanswered

The cold weather outside,
But a warm storm inside.

"How did you land up here?"
Asked my heart, in fear.

Is it because of someone,
Or for someone?
Yet to be answered!

My heart longs for answers,
Yet all in vain—
Waiting for the moment
When clarity will dawn upon my soul,
To finally serve my life well.

Us

The glowing visages—
Upshot of the radiant rays,
With a grin like a Cheshire cat,
Never meant to fade away!

This feeling tickles me,
A gift from thee.
A moment of delight,
Cherished to the greatest height!

Seal a promise
To be together—
No matter the distance,
You'll be here forever!

The poems in **Never Again** lead us through an intimate landscape of memory, resilience, and transformation. These pieces are more than explorations of love and loss; they are windows into the human experience, capturing both the ache of farewell and the quiet strength that follows.

Each poem invites readers to confront their own truths, to find beauty in moments of vulnerability, and to celebrate the courage it takes to let go and begin anew. As we journey through these verses, we are reminded that while "never again" may feel final, it often marks the start of a new path forward.

Thank you for embarking on this journey — may these words linger in your heart as a testament to the power of reflection and renewal.

www.ingramcontent.com/pod-product-compliance
Lightning Source LLC
LaVergne TN
LVHW041754190726
843493LV00008B/2625